In the Beginning God
Created the Earth...

the Small Plants

The Bible Tells Me So Press

In the Beginning God Created the Earth...
the Small Plants

A children's book produced by
The Bible Tells Me So Press

Copyright © 2021
The Bible Tells Me So Corporation

All rights reserved. No part of this book, neither text nor illustrations, may be reproduced without permission in writing by the publisher.

PUBLISHED BY
THE BIBLE TELLS ME SO CORPORATION
WWW.THEBIBLETELLSMESO.COM

First Printing, November 2021

God made
the small
plants.

They didn't just happen by chance or by accident.

and the herbs
and spices
that we enjoy
were all made by God
for us.

that cover a little less than half the land on earth.

Much of what we eat comes from grass. Bread, sugar, rice, and even corn come from different kinds of grass.

And we benefit from grass in a lot of other ways. For example...

cows and other animals eat a lot of grass.

Then they
   turn it into the milk
      that we drink
      and the meat
   that we eat.

Grass also helps keep the dirt and soil in place when it rains.

If it weren't for all the tiny grass roots
that take a good hold
of the soil, the dirt would
be carried away.

Then, there are
the beautiful flowers.

Flowers are a wonderful source of food for many different kinds of insects, birds, and animals as well as for humans.

When bees
or other kinds of insects
come to feed on
a flower's nectar,

they get
pollen caught
on their legs and
carry it with them
when they fly away.

This helps the flowers to spread and grow in many other places.

Flowers not only look beautiful, they also smell lovely.

They help make the world a beautiful, colorful, and fragrant place to live.

People have been using herbs and spices for thousands of years.

We use them to make medicines to help us get better when we feel sick.

And spices, like these mint leaves, are fragrant and delicious.

So, the next time you play on a beautiful grassy field,

admire some lovely flowers,

have a delightful tea party, or enjoy a delicious cupcake,

take a moment to stop and give the Lord a big thank You

He causes the grass
to grow for the cattle,
and herbage for man's use,
that he may bring forth food
from the earth.

Psalm 104:14

For more
books, videos, songs, and crafts,
visit us online at
TheBibleTellsMeSo.com

Standing on the Bible and growing!

www.ingramcontent.com/pod-product-compliance
Lightning Source LLC
Chambersburg PA
CBHW042124040426
42450CB00002B/60